The Histroy of Taisekiji

Taho Fuji Dainichirenge-zan Taisekiji was founded on October 12th in the third year of Sho'o (1290) by Second High Priest, Byakuren Ajari Nikko Shonin, the legitimate successor to our Founder Nichiren Daishonin. The name Taisekiji is derived from the name of the area, Oishi-ga-hara (*"Oishi"* is another way to pronounce the Chinese characters for *"Taiseki"*). The founding lord, Nanjo Shichiro Jiro Taira-no Tokimitsu (commonly known as "Nanjo Tokimitsu"), was the lord of Fuji Ueno County. In the fifth year of Ko'an (1282), Nikko Shonin received the transmission of the entirety of Nichiren Daishonin's Buddhism. After the Daishonin's passing, he became the Chief Priest (*betto*) of Minobu-san Kuonji Temple. Within a few years, however, at the instigation of Mimbu Ajari Niko, Hakiri Sanenaga, the lord of the area, began to repeatedly commit slanderous acts against the Daishonin's teachings. Nikko Shonin frequently gave Sanenaga strict admonitions to put a halt to his slanderous behavior. Sanenaga, however, ignored his master and refused to correct it. Nichiren Daishonin had previously stated in his will, "When the lord of Mount Minobu goes against the Law, I (Nichiren) will no longer reside there." Furthermore, in one of his final directives, the Daishonin stated, "When the sovereign embraces this Law, establish the [True] High Sanctuary of Hommonji Temple at Mount Fuji." Thus, Nikko Shonin decided to leave Mount Minobu in the spring of the second year of Sho'o (1289), carrying with him the foundation of true Buddhism, the Dai-Gohonzon of the High Sanctuary of the Essential Teaching, together with the ashes of Nichiren Daishonin. He also took the Goshos, which are the original writings of Nichiren Daishonin, some of the Daishonin's belongings, and other sacred treasures. Nikko Shonin moved to Fuji at the request of Nichiren Daishonin's staunch believer, Nanjo Tokimitsu. In the following year, the third year of Sho'o (1290), Nikko Shonin established the foundation of Taisekiji, where he enshrined the Dai-Gohonzon, trained many disciples, and constructed the foundation for the perpetuity of the propagation of true Buddhism. Since that time, for more than 700 years, Taisekiji has been continuously transmitting true Buddhism of our Founder, Nichiren Daishonin without any interruption.

Index

The History of Taisekiji / 1
Map of Taisekiji / 3
① Hoando / 4
② Somon / Kuromon (Main Gate) / 8
③ Sammon *(Gate of Three Entrances)* / 10
④ Tatchu Sando *(Pilgrimage Path along the Lodging Temples)* / 12
   Chuo Tatchu *(Central Lodging Temple Buildings)* / 14
⑤ Renzobo / ① Jorembo / ② Rikyobo / ③ Kujobo / ④ Hyakkambo /
   ⑤ Rentobo / ⑥ Jakunichibo / ⑦ Honjubo / ⑧ Kangyobo / ⑨ Honkyobo /
   ⑩ Renjobo / ⑪ Ryoshobo / ⑫ Minaminobo
   Higashi tatchu *(Eastern Lodging Temple Buildings)* / 16
   ⑯ Myo'ombo / ⑰ Ho'ombo / ⑱ Onshimbo / ⑲ Higashinobo / ⑳ Honshubo /
⑥ Sessembo / ⑦ Renyo'an / ⑧ Fujimian
⑨ Ishinobo and Joshodo *(Ever-chanting Temple)* / 18
⑩ Seppo-ishi *(Boulder for the Preaching of the Law)* / 19
⑪ Tahozo *(Storehouse of Many Treasures)* / 19
⑫ Hoshoen *(Hoshoen Garden)* / 20
   Nishi tatchu *(Western Lodging Temple Buildings)* / 22
   ㉑ Myosembo / ㉒ Myojubo / ㉓ Onjubo
⑬ Nitemmon *(Gate of Two Heavens of the Sun and Moon)* / 22
⑭ Mieido *(Image Hall)* / 24
⑮ Koro *(Drum Tower)* and ⑯ Shoro *(Bell Tower)* / 27
⑰ Rokuman-to *(Tower of the Sixty-thousand)* / 28
⑱ Atsuwara sanretsushi-hi *(Monument to the Three Atsuwara Martyrs)* / 28
⑲ Onimon *(Demon Gate)* / 28
⑳ Kyakuden *(Reception Hall)* / 30
㉑ Akazu-no-mon *(Unopened Gate)* / 33
㉒ Mutsubo / 34
㉓ Gohozo *(Treasure Storehouse)* / 36
㉔ Daishoin *(Great Writing Hall)* / 37
㉕ Daibo and Naiji-bu *(Internal Affairs Department)* / 38
㉖ Shumuin-chosha *(Nichiren Shoshu Head Office Building)* / 38
㉗ Dai-kodo *(Great Lecture Hall)* / 39
㉘ Chu-kodo *(Medium-Sized Lecture Hall)* / 40
㉙ Uramon *(Rear Gate)* / 41
㉚ Goju-no-to *(Five-storied Pagoda)* / 42
㉛ Okyozo *(Sutra Storehouse)* / 44
㉜ Junikakudo *(Twelve-sided Temple)* / 45
㉝ Ohanamizu *(Water-drawing Place)* and Akado *(Spring Water House)* / 45
㉞ Kofubo / 46
㉟ Soichibo and ㊱ Sonibo / 48
㊲ Joraibo / ㊳ Tozan Jimusho *(Tozan Office)* / ㊴ Tokohibo / 50
㊵ Myogobo / ㊶ Hogobo / ㊷ Jorakubo / 51
   Senyokudo (㊸ East / ㊹ West) / ㊺ Kannedo / 52
㊻ Taisekiji Bochi *(Taisekiji Cemetery)* / ㊼ Tenrei-in / 53
㊽ Dai-nokotsudo *(Grand Cinerarium)* / 54
㊾ Daimyo Bochi *(Cemetery of Feudal Lords)* / 55
Transportation Guide Map for the Head Temple Vicinity / 56

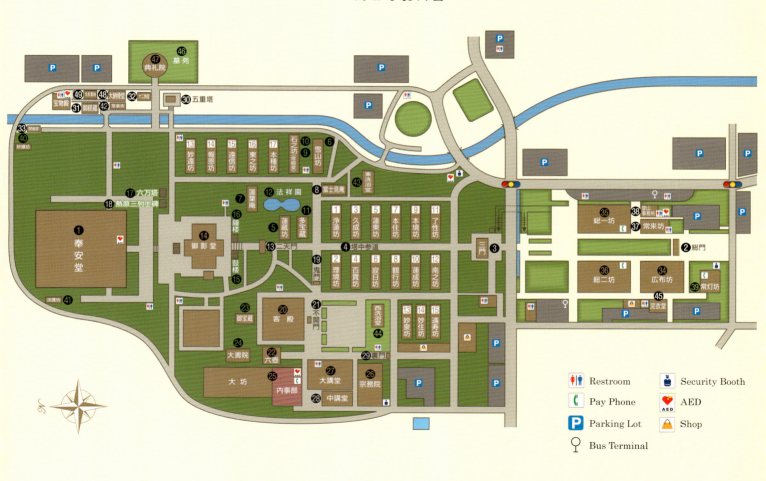

Hoando 奉安堂

The Hoando was completed in October of 2002 based on the initial aspiration of Sixty-seventh High Priest Nikken Shonin as part of the great undertaking to commemorate the 750th Anniversary of the Establishment of True Buddhism. It is the worship hall where the Dai-Gohonzon of the High Sanctuary of the Essential Teaching is enshrined. The exterior structure was constructed in the traditional Japanese temple style with a two-story pyramidal roof. It houses a ground floor and basement, and is constructed with a steel-frame and partly in reinforced concrete. The imposing structure measures 75 meters in width, 116 meters in length, and has a height of 55 meters. It is comparatively the largest structure built in the traditional Japanese architectural style. The main hall of the Hoando measures 55 meters in width and 84 meters in length. More than 230 tatami mats provide seating for priests in the Inner Sanctuary, while chairs for more than 5,000 believers are installed in the Outer Sanctuary to offer unobstructed views of the Dai-Gohonzon. The altar, where the Dai-Gohonzon is enshrined, functions as a storehouse made of special alloy to ensure maximum security.

Interior of the Hoando

Front view of the roof of the Hoando with cherry blossoms

Chinese gable

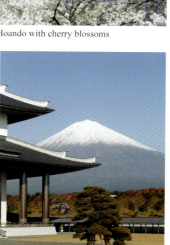

Ridge and end tiles   View of Mount Fuji from Shoshintei Garden

Hoando blanketed in snow

Somon *(Main Gate)* 総門

The Somon Gate *(Main Gate)* is located at the southern-most entrance to the temple grounds. Lacquered in black, it has commonly been called the Kuromon Gate *(Black Gate)* since ancient times. Taisekiji's historical records show that the Somon Gate was built in the second year of Dai'ei (1522) by Twelfth High Priest Nitchin Shonin. However, the current gate was reconstructed in 1880 by Fifty-fifth High Priest Nippu Shonin to commemorate the 600th Anniversary of the Passing of our Founder, Nichiren Daishonin and the 550th Anniversary of the Passing of Second High Priest Nikko Shonin and Third High Priest Nichimoku Shonin. In 1998, during maintenance and improvements to the surrounding area, the Black Gate was moved from its previous location on the south side of the Soichibo to its current location as the main entrance to Head Temple Taisekiji.

Sammon *(Gate of Three Entrances)* 三門

Approximately 400 meters north of the Somon Gate stands a towering structure, the Sammon Gate *(Gate of Three Entrances)*. The red lacquered wooden gate, with proportions of almost 24 meters wide, 11 meters deep and a height of 22 meters, is the largest of its kind in Japan's Tokai region and the pinnacle of magnificent beauty. The construction work of the gate began under the auspices of Twenty-fifth High Priest Nichiyu Shonin. At that time, the Sixth Tokugawa Shogun, Ienobu donated 70 giant trees from Mt. Fuji, and in the second year of Shotoku (1712) his wife, Tennei-in-den contributed 1,200 pieces of gold for its construction. It took six years to build and was completed in the second year of Kyoho (1717). Minor repairs have since been made. In 1966, the Sammon Gate was designated by the Government of Shizuoka Prefecture as a Prefectural Tangible Cultural Asset.

Eaves and colonnades on the north side of the Sammon Gate

Tatchu Sando *(Pilgrimage Path Lined by the Lodging Temples)* 塔中参道

When one walks along the Tatchu Sando *(Pilgrimage Path Lined by the Lodging Temple)* from the Sammon Gate to the Mieido, one sees that the wide path is paved with stones, and that spring water from Mt. Fuji runs along both sides. With the coming of spring, the entire avenue is brilliantly colored as weeping cherry trees on both sides of the Pilgrimage Path burst into bloom. The stone pavement has been widened a number of times throughout the years to accommodate the greatly increased numbers of believers coming on tozan pilgrimages. Likewise, repairs to the stone walls have been made, offering a beautiful scene of graceful landscaping.

The Pilgrimage Path colored in cherry blossoms at night

Weeping cherry trees and spring water stream

Chuo Tatchu *(Central Lodging Temple Buildings)* 中央塔中

Renzobo 蓮蔵坊

Third High Priest Nichimoku Shonin built the Renzobo in the third year of Sho'o (1290), and in the second year of Hoei (1705), Twenty-fourth High Priest Nichiei Shonin rebuilt it as living quarters for the Chief Instructor of the Priests *(Gakuto)*. The reconstruction of the present building was completed in 1981 by Sixty-seventh High Priest Nikken Shonin for the 700th Anniversary of the Passing of Nichiren Daishonin.

Jorembo 浄蓮坊

The Jorembo was founded in the first year of Genko (1331) by Hoki Ajari Nichido Shonin (later, the Fourth High Priest), a disciple of Nichimoku Shonin. The reconstruction of the present building was completed in 2007 by Sixty-eighth High Priest Nichinyo Shonin as part of the great undertaking for the 750th Anniversary of Revealing the Truth and Upholding Justice through the Submission of the *Rissho ankoku-ron* (On Securing the Peace of the Land through the Propagation of True Buddhism).

Rikyobo 理境坊

The Rikyobo was founded in the third year of Sho'o (1290) by Shimotsuke Ajari Nisshu, a disciple of Nikko Shonin. The reconstruction of the present building was completed in 1977; and in 1990, additions and improvements were made to commemorate the 700th Anniversary of the Founding of Taisekiji.

Kujobo 久成坊

The Kujobo was founded in the third year of Sho'o (1290) by Tamano Taifu Ajari Nichizon, a disciple of Nichimoku Shonin. The reconstruction of the present building was completed in 2007 by Sixty-eighth High Priest Nichinyo Shonin as part of the great undertaking for the 750th Anniversary of Revealing the Truth and Upholding Justice through the Submission of the *Rissho ankoku-ron*.

Hyakkambo 百貫坊

Originally called Jorembo, the Hyakkambo was founded in the third year of Sho'o (1290) by Settsu Ajari Nissen, a disciple of Nikko Shonin. The reconstruction of the present building was completed in 2008 by Sixty-eighth High Priest Nichinyo Shonin as part of the great undertaking for the 750th Anniversary of Revealing the Truth and Upholding Justice through the Submission of the *Rissho ankoku-ron*.

Rentobo 蓮東坊

The Rentobo was founded in the second year of Einin (1294) by Mikawa-ko Nichizo, a disciple of Nichimoku Shonin. The reconstruction of the present building was completed in 2007 by Sixty-eighth High Priest Nichinyo Shonin as part of the great undertaking for the 750th Anniversary of Revealing the Truth and Upholding Justice through the Submission of the *Rissho ankoku-ron*.

Jakunichibo 寂日坊

Jakunichi-bo was founded in the third year of Sho'o (1290) by Jakunichi-bo Nikke, a disciple of Nikko Shonin. Since ancient times, it has been the main Tatchu building that serves as an official center. Its vermillion-lacquered gate reveals its significance. The present building completed its reconstruction in 1984 by Sixty-seventh High Priest Nikken Shonin.

Honjubo 本住坊

The Honjubo was founded in the second year of Engen (1337) by Kunaikyo Ajari Nichigyo Shonin (later, the Fifth High Priest), a disciple of Fourth High Priest Nichido Shonin. The reconstruction of the present building was completed in 2008 by Sixty-eighth High Priest Nichinyo Shonin as part of the great undertaking for the 750th Anniversary of Revealing the Truth and Upholding Justice through the Submission of the *Rissho ankoku-ron*.

Kangyobo 観行坊

The Kangyobo was founded in the first year of Geno (1319) by Ise-ko Nichien, a disciple of Nichimoku Shonin. The reconstruction of the present building was completed in 2008 by Sixty-eighth High Priest Nichinyo Shonin as part of the great undertaking for the 750th Anniversary of Revealing the Truth and Upholding Justice through the Submission of the *Rissho ankoku-ron*.

Honkyobo 本境坊

Originally called Jibubo, the Honkyobo was founded in the first year of Genko (1321) by Jibu-ko Nichien, a disciple of Nikko Shonin. The reconstruction of the present building was completed in 2008 by Sixty-eighth High Priest Nichinyo Shonin as part of the great undertaking for the 750th Anniversary of Revealing the Truth and Upholding Justice through the Submission of the *Rissho ankoku-ron*.

Renjobo 蓮成坊

Originally called Jokambo, the Renjobo was founded in the first year of Shoan (1299) by Echigo-bo Nichiben, a disciple of Nikko Shonin. The reconstruction of the present building was completed in 2008 by Sixty-eighth High Priest Nichinyo Shonin as part of the great undertaking for the 750th Anniversary of Revealing the Truth and Upholding Justice through the Submission of the *Rissho ankoku-ron*.

Higashi Tatchu (Eastern Lodging Temple Buildings) 東塔中

Ryoshobo 了性坊
The Ryoshobo was founded in the fourth year of Einin (1296) by Daigaku Ryosho-bo Nichijo, a disciple of Nikko Shonin. It was originally called Rensembo and was located on the north side of the Renzobo. However, it was moved to its present location at the time of Seventeenth High Priest Nissei Shonin. The reconstruction of the present building was completed in 1986 by Sixty-seventh High Priest Nikken Shonin.

Myo'ombo 妙遠坊
The Myo'ombo was founded in March of 1964 by Sixty-sixth High Priest Nittatsu Shonin. It was originally built where the Onjubo is presently located. It was rebuilt when moved to its present location in 2008 by Sixty-eighth High Priest Nichinyo Shonin as part of the great undertaking for the 750th Anniversary of Revealing the Truth and Upholding Justice through the Submission of the *Rissho ankoku-ron*.

Ho'ombo 報恩坊
The Ho'ombo was founded in the fifth year of Genbun (1740) by Thirtieth High Priest Nicchu Shonin. It was built anew by Sixty-seventh High Priest Nikken Shonin as part of the project to commemorate the 700th Anniversary of the Founding of Taisekiji.

Minaminobo 南之坊
The Minaminobo was founded in the third year of Sho'o (1290) by Sho'u-bo Nichizen, a disciple of Nikko Shonin. It was originally called Sho'ubo and was located on north side of the Rikyobo. However, it was moved to its present location at the time of Seventeenth High Priest Nissei Shonin. The reconstruction of the present building was completed in 2008 by Sixty-eighth High Priest Nichinyo Shonin as part of the great undertaking for the 750th Anniversary of Revealing the Truth and Upholding Justice through the Submission of the *Rissho ankoku-ron*.

Onshimbo 遠信坊
The Onshimbo was founded by Onshin-bo Nichigu during the Genroku period (between 1688 and 1703) and built anew in 1963 by Sixty-sixth High Priest Nittatsu Shonin. The reconstruction of the present building was completed in 2007 by Sixty-eighth High Priest Nichinyo Shonin as part of the great undertaking for the 750th Anniversary of Revealing the Truth and Upholding Justice through the Submission of the *Rissho ankoku-ron*.

Higashinobo 東之坊

The Higashinobo was founded in the second year of Eikyo (1745) by Thirty-first High Priest Nichiin Shonin, and built anew in 1955 by Sixty-fourth High Priest Nissho Shonin. The reconstruction of the present building was completed in 2008 by Sixty-eighth High Priest Nichinyo Shonin as part of the great undertaking for the 750th Anniversary of Revealing the Truth and Upholding Justice through the Submission of the *Rissho ankoku-ron*.

Honshubo 本種坊

The Honshubo was founded in 1961 by Sixty-sixth High Priest Nittatsu Shonin. The reconstruction of the present building was completed in 2008 by Sixty-eighth High Priest Nichinyo Shonin as part of the great undertaking for the 750th Anniversary of Revealing the Truth and Upholding Justice through the Submission of the *Rissho ankoku-ron*.

Sessembo 雪山坊

The Sessembo was founded in 1926 by Fifty-ninth High Priest Nichiko Shonin. The reconstruction of the present building was completed in 2008 by Sixty-eighth High Priest Nichinyo Shonin as part of the great undertaking for the 750th Anniversary of Revealing the Truth and Upholding Justice through the Submission of the *Rissho ankoku-ron*.

Renyo'an 蓮葉庵

Called the Renyo'an, this residence was built by Fifty-second High Priest Nichiden Shonin on the ancient site of the Jumyobo. The reconstruction of the present building was completed in 1990 by Sixty-seventh High Priest Nikken Shonin as a part of the project to commemorate the 700th Anniversary of the Founding of Head Temple Taisekiji.

Fujimian 富士見庵

The Fujimian building was originally founded during the Genroku period (around 1700) on the north side of the Ishinobo. The present building was newly constructed in 1958 at its current location by Sixty-fifth High Priest Nichijun Shonin. A number of repairs have since been made to the building.

Ishinobo and Joshodo
(Ever-chanting Temple) 石之坊（常唱堂）

The Ishinobo was founded in the ninth year of Kyoho (1724) by Twenty-sixth High Priest Nichikan Shonin. He furthermore constructed the Joshodo *(Ever-chanting Temple)* in the eleventh year of Kyoho (1726). It is also called the Jo-daimoku-do *(Ever-chanting-Daimoku Temple)*, because in its beginnings, it is said that Daimoku was unceasingly chanted day and night by six priests. The Joshodo building was relocated as the main hall of the Ishinobo in 1925 by Fifty-eighth High Priest Nitchu Shonin, and, in 1966, Sixty-sixth High Priest Nittatsu Shonin rebuilt them as a structure housing a square hall measuring approximately 11 meters on all sides.

Tahozo *(Storehouse of Many Treasures)* 多宝蔵

The Tahozo *(Storehouse of Many Treasures)* was built to the west of Hoshoen Garden in 1990 to commemorate the 700th Anniversary of the Founding of Head Temple Taisekiji. The building is fire-resistant, seismically retrofitted and is constructed in an ancient architectural style utilizing intercrossed triangle logs *(azekura-zukuri)*. The building houses many of Taisekiji's treasured ancient writings.

Seppo-ishi *(Boulder for the Preaching of the Law)* 説法石

From the time that Nikko Shonin moved to the Fuji Ueno area until the time when Taisekiji was constructed, it is said that he often preached the true Law to people from the top of this boulder, located on the current site of the Ishinobo.

Hoshoen 法祥園

The spacious Hoshoen Garden measures approximately 5,300 square meters (1.3 acres) and was completed on the south side of the Renyo'an in 1990 as one of the projects to commemorate the 700th Anniversary of the Founding of Head Temple Taisekiji. On clear days, magnificent Mount Fuji is vividly reflected in the Myokyo-ike *(Bright Mirror Pond)*, situated in the center of the garden.

View from the north side of the Hoshoen Garden

Nishi Tatchu (Western Lodging Temple Buildings) 西塔中

Myosembo 妙泉坊
The Myosembo was founded in 1969 by Sixty-sixth High Priest Nittatsu Shonin. The reconstruction of the present building was completed in 2008 by Sixty-eighth High Priest Nichinyo Shonin as part of the great undertaking for the 750th Anniversary of Revealing the Truth and Upholding Justice through the Submission of the *Rissho ankoku-ron*.

Myojubo 妙住坊
The Myojubo was founded in 1969 by Sixty-sixth High Priest Nittatsu Shonin. The reconstruction of the present building was completed in 2008 by Sixty-eighth High Priest Nichinyo Shonin as part of the great undertaking for the 750th Anniversary of Revealing the Truth and Upholding Justice through the Submission of the *Rissho ankoku-ron*.

Onjubo 遠寿坊
The Onjubo was founded in 1978 by Sixty-sixth High Priest Nittatsu Shonin in commemoration of the 700th Anniversary of the Passing of Nichiren Daishonin. The building was originally located on the west side of the Myosembo. It was moved to its present location and reconstructed in 2008 by Sixty-eighth High Priest Nichinyo Shonin as part of the great undertaking for the 750th Anniversary of Revealing the Truth and Upholding Justice through the Submission of the *Rissho ankoku-ron*.

Nitemmon (Gate of Two Heavens of the Sun and Moon) 二天門

The red-lacquered Nitemmon Gate *(Gate of Two Heavens of the Sun and Moon)* is located near the mid-point of the Tatchu Sando between the Sammon Gate and the Mieido. Therefore, it has also been called the Nakamon Gate *(Middle Gate)*. According to Taisekiji's recorded history, it was first built in the 15th year of Kan'ei (1638) by Seventeenth High Priest Nissei Shonin. The present structure was rebuilt during the time of Sixty-sixth High Priest Nittatsu Shonin in 1960. As part of the great undertaking for the 800th Anniversary of the Advent of ouf Founder Nichiren Daishonin, the gate was renovated by Sixth-eighth High Priest Nichinyo Shonin, and the renovation work was completed in November 2017.

Mieido *(Image Hall)* 御影堂

When making one's way northward on the Tatchu Sando, one will find the Mieido *(Image Hall)*, a red-lacquered building. It is also commonly known as "*Mido.*" An image of Nichiren Daishonin, reverently carved by Echizen Hokkyo Kai'e in the second year of Kakei (1388) at the time of Sixth High Priest Nichiji Shonin, is enshrined within the altar. The Mieido was first founded by Second High Priest Nikko Shonin. The present structure was reconstructed in the ninth year of Kan'ei (1632) during the time of Seventeenth High Priest Nissei Shonin, with an offering from Kyodai-in-den, the wife of Hachisuka Yoshishige-ko, Lord of the Awa-Tokushima Domain. The building measures 25 meters in width, and 23 meters in both depth and height. In 1966, it was declared a Tangible Cultural Asset of Shizuoka Prefecture. As part of the great undertaking for the 750th Anniversary of Revealing the Truth and Upholding Justice through the Submission of the *Rissho ankoku-ron*, the building was entirely taken apart for the major revovation by Sixth-eighth High Priest Nichinyo Shonin, and after seven years of construction work, it was completed in Novermber 2013.

The altar of the Mieido

Outer Sanctuary of the Mieido

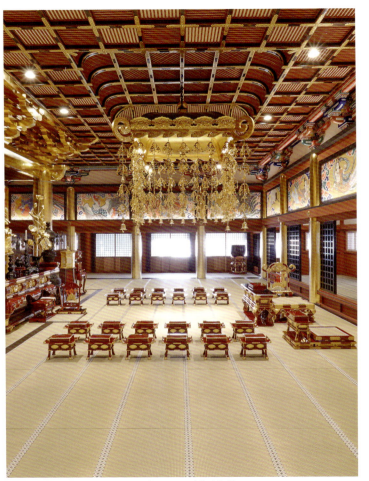
Inner Sanctuary of the Mieido

Koro *(Drum Tower)* and Shoro *(Bell Tower)* 鼓楼・鐘楼

The Koro *(Drum Tower)* and Shoro *(Bell Tower)* stand on the southwest and southeast sides of the Mieido building. Their location may give the appearance that the Pilgrimage Path runs between the Drum Tower and Bell Tower. They were founded in the beginning of the Edo period (1615-1868) by Seventeenth High Priest Nissei Shonin. The reconstruction of the present buildings was completed in 1990 by Sixty-seventh High Priest Nikken Shonin in commemoration of the 700th Anniversary of the Founding of Head Temple Taisekiji. The drum is beaten from the Drum Tower as the High Priest enters the Mieido to officiate at ceremonies. In contrast, the large bell in the Bell Tower is chimed three times a day—in the morning and evening, and at noon. It is also sounded during grand ceremonies and on New Year's Eve.

The Koro *(Drum Tower)*

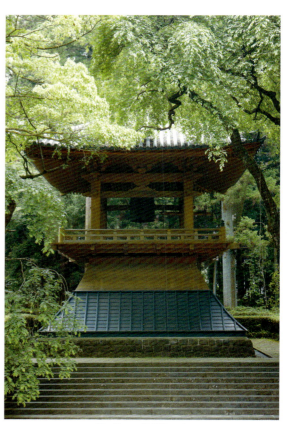

The Shoro *(Bell Tower)*

Rokuman-to
(Tower of the Sixty-thousand) 六万塔

Two monuments signifying the Rokuman-to *(Tower of the Sixty-thousand)* stand on the east side of the Kokaimon Gate (Wide Open Gate) of the Hoando. To the right stands the older tower, which was constructed in the first year of Ho'ei (1704) at the time of Twenty-fourth High Priest Nichiei Shonin, resulting from the six million Daimoku chanted by lay believers of the Suruga, Musashi, Kaga, Kyoto, Osaka and Awa areas. The newer tower to the left was constructed in 1994 at the time of Sixty-seventh High Priest Nikken Shonin, resulting from six hundred million Daimoku chanted by priests and lay believers throughout the world. Both hexogonal towers represent Bodhisattva Jogyo followed by the bodhisattvas of the sands of sixty thousand Ganges Rivers who emerged from the earth to propagate Myoho-Renge-Kyo in the Latter Day of the Law on the occasion of the Emerging from the Earth *(Juji yujutsu;* fifteenth) chapter of the Lotus Sutra preached by Shakyamuni Buddha in India.

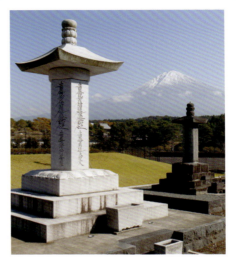

Onimon (Demon Gate)
鬼門

Walking up the Tatchu Sando past the central lodging temple buildings, and turning left down a small path toward the Kyakuden, one reaches the Onimon Gate *(Demon Gate)*. This gate, erected in the ancient Chinese gabled-roof style, is so called because of the demon mask at its top ("*Oni*" means "*Demon*" in Japanese). It is considered the front gate of the Daibo. Constructed by Twenty-fifth High Priest Nichiyu Shonin in the second year of Kyoho (1717), the Onimon Gate is said to be a symbol of conversion to true Buddhism. As part of the great undertaking for the 800th Anniversary of the Advent of ouf Founder Nichiren Daishonin, the gate was renovated by Sixth-eighth High Priest Nichinyo Shonin, and the renovation work was completed in December 2016.

Atsuwara sanretsushi-hi (Monument to the Three Atsuwara Martyrs) 熱原三烈士碑

This memorial monument was erected to honor the three martyrs including Jinshiro, who courageously followed true Buddhism to their martyrdom during the Atsuwara Persecution in the second year of Ko'an (1279).

28

Kyakuden *(Reception Hall)* 客殿

The Kyakuden *(Reception Hall)* is one of the central structures where the majority of ceremonies at the Head Temple are held. These include Ushitora Gongyo, the prayer for the achievement of kosen-rufu, conducted every morning by each successive High Priest, the recipient of the Heritage of the Law since the time of Nichiren Daishonin. The Kyakuden was originally built in the sixth year of Kansho (1465) by Ninth High Priest Nichiu Shonin. Reconstructed a number of times since its original construction, it was newly rebuilt in 1998 by Sixty-seventh High Priest Nikken Shonin. The basic structure is made of steel, and the building exterior and interior finishes are entirely of natural wood forming a warm, traditional Japanese-style structure. It measures 50 meters in width as well as in depth, and its two-stories reach a height of 36 meters. The Kyakuden provides a large space, equipped with 1,112 tatami mats.

The Kyakuden at dawn

The interior of the Kyakuden

Plaque on the front steps

Eastern corridor

Cloud Gong hung at the west side of the Kyakuden

Front of the Kyakuden with cherry blossoms in full bloom

Akazu-no-mon *(Unopened Gate)*
不開門

The small gate, which stands in front of the Kyakuden is called the Akazu-no-mon Gate *(Unopened Gate)*, and is also referred to as the "Chokushi-mon" *(Emperor's Messenger Gate)*. Akazu-no-mon ("*Akazu*" means "*unopened*" in Japanese) is so called because it is to remain firmly closed until the dawning of kosen-rufu, when it is to be opened. It is not certain when the gate was originally constructed, but records show that it was rebuilt during the time of Twenty-fourth High Priest Nichiei Shonin in the middle of the Edo period (1615-1868). The current Akazu-no-mon Gate was newly rebuilt by Sixty-seventh High Priest Nikken Shonin in time for the reconstruction of the Reception Hall in 1998.

Mutsubo 六壺

The Mutsubo is located to the west of the Kyakuden. Founded by Second High Priest Nikko Shonin, it is said that the Mutsubo is so called because when it was first built, it was divided into six rooms ("*Mutsu*" means "*six*" in Japanese). It functions as the "dojo" for morning and evening Gongyo for priests in training. In October of 1988, the present Mutsubo was completely rebuilt by Sixty-seventh High Priest Nikken Shonin in commemoration of the 700th Anniversary of the Founding of Taisekiji. Constructed completely of zelkova wood, with a concave pyramidal roof made of hand-crafted ceramic tiles and earthen walls finished with stucco, the single-story earthquake-resistant structure is in the traditional ancient wooden architectural style, and measures approximately 18 meters on each side. Additionally, this completely-wooden structure equipped with 170 tatami mats contains only four supporting pillars, because construction was carefully considered so that all the priests and lay participants would be able to chant to the Gohonzon with an unobstructed view. The Mutsubo was presented with a special award by the Architectural Technology Association.

Interior of the Mutsubo

Waterfall in front of the Mutsubo

Gohozo *(Treasure Storehouse)*
御宝蔵

Surrounded by Japanese cedar trees, the Gohozo *(Treasure Storehouse)* stands on the north side of the Kyakuden. Measuring 7.2 meters in width and 9 meters from front to rear, it is built in the "storehouse" style, roofed with copper shingles and bordered by a moat. Carefully protected within its confines are Gohonzons inscribed by the Founder Nichiren Daishonin, treasures including original writings by Nichiren Daishonin such as, *On Remonstrating with Hachiman* (*Kangyo hachiman-sho*) and *Reply to Nanjo* (*Nanjo dono-gohenji*), which have been nationally designated as Important Cultural Assets, and Gohonzons transcribed by successive High Priests. During the spring "Airing of the Sacred Treasures Ceremony" *(Goreiho mushibarai-daihoe)*, the lay believers who attend it are permitted to witness these sacred treasures as they are aired to prevent damage by insects. The oldest records state that the first storehouse was constructed by Ninth High Priest Nichiu Shonin, and that Thirty-seventh High Priest Nippo Shonin had the storehouse rebuilt in the second year of Kansei (1790) in its current style. It has been repaired a few times since its reconstruction.

Chinese gable

Daishoin *(Great Writing Hall)* 大書院

The Daishoin *(Great Writing Hall)* is an elegant structure built in the Japanese style to the northeast of the Kyakuden. In general, Writing Hall, or "*Shoin*" in Japanese, is the place to be used for lectures and receiving guests. This building is said to have been built at the beginning of the Edo period (1615-1868). In October of 1981, it was completely rebuilt in the present style by Sixty-seventh High Priest Nikken Shonin in commemoration of the 700th Anniversary of the Passing of Nichiren Daishonin. The Great Writing Hall is constructed with white walls and blond wood. Its pyramidal roof, with eaves that upturn, is finished with wide, rectangular, copper-plated shingles. The interior affords the building a spacious 198 tatami mat writing hall.

View of the Daishoin over Japanese apricot trees blooming with red blossoms

The front entrance

Spaciousness of the hall of the Daishoin seen in the morning sunshine

Daibo and Naiji-bu *(Internal Affairs Department)* 大坊（内事部）

The Daibo, located to the west of the Mutsubo, is the central building of Taisekiji where the successive High Priests have lived since it was originally built in the third year of Sho'o (1290) by Second High Priest Nikko Shonin. During the time of the Sixty-sixth High Priest Nittatsu Shonin in 1962, the present structure was completely rebuilt, and consists of the Naiji-bu (*Internal Affairs Department*), which administrates all operations of Head Temple Taisekiji's vast grounds, the cinerarium storage request office, the toba memorial service request office, executive offices, conference rooms, dormitories for the priests in training, lodgings for the priests from local temples, the main dining hall, and kitchens.

Shumuin Chosha *(Nichiren Shoshu Head Office Building)* 宗務院庁舎

The Nichiren Shoshu Head Office Building (*Shumuin chosha*) stands directly to the south of the Dai-kodo. It houses the various offices that manage the administration of Nichiren Shoshu, revering Taisekiji as the Head Temple. In 1981, as part of the project to commemorate the 700th Anniversary of the Passing of Nichiren Daishonin, it was newly built by Sixty-seventh High Priest Nikken Shonin. The modern structure built with steel-reinforced concrete has an area of 2,500 square meters. The first floor houses department offices, a reception room, a lobby, and a storage area. The second floor consists of the executive director's room, department offices, conference rooms, and the kitchen.

Dai-kodo *(Great Lecture Hall)* 大講堂

The Dai-kodo *(Great Lecture Hall)*, standing to the south of the Daibo, was built at the time of Sixty-fifth High Priest Nichijun Shonin in 1958. The seven-story structure, made of steel reinforced concrete, has a total floor space of 9,240 square meters. Rooms for meetings and classrooms for the Fuji Gakurin (school for the Nichiren Shoshu priesthood) are at the north end, and the third through sixth stories at the south end collectively serve as a spacious 702 tatami mat auditorium. The Dai-kodo is used for the diligent pursuit of doctrinal studies and receiving propagation lectures for great numbers of priests and lay believers.

Spacious auditorium of the Dai-kodo

Chu-kodo *(Medium-sized Lecture Hall)* 中講堂

The Chu-kodo *(Medium-sized Lecture Hall)*, located on the west side of the Dai-kodo, was built in 1988 as part of the project to commemorate the 700th Anniversary of the Founding of the Head Temple. This three-story structure is made of steel-reinforced concrete. The first floor has a reception room, conference room and parking facilities. The Fuji Gakurin Library on the second floor houses library stacks, a reading room, study room and others. The entire third floor serves as a 300-person capacity auditorium.

Uramon *(Rear Gate)* 裏門

Standing at the southern end of the path in front of the Mutsubo is a gate called the Uramon Gate *(Rear Gate)*, in contrast with the Onimon Gate which stands as the front gate of the Daibo. It is not certain when the gate was originally constructed, however, this gate is shown in the *Illustrations of Taiksekiji* (Taisekiji ezu) published in the middle of the Edo Period (1615-1868), where it is recorded that it was newly rebuilt at the time of Forty-ninth High Priest Nissho Shonin in the sixth year of Bunsei (1823). The present gate was reconstructed in 1988 by Sixty-seventh High Priest Nikken Shonin as part of the project to commemorate the 700th Anniversary of the Founding of the Head Temple, measuring 7.5 meters in width, 4 meters from front to rear and 6.5 meters in height.

Goju-no-to
(Five-storied Pagoda) 五重塔

Surrounded by trees, the Goju-no-to *(Five-storied Pagoda)* stands on a hill on the far side of the Uruigawa River, facing west. It is said to be the finest pagoda on the Tokaido, the ancient road that links Tokyo and Kyoto. The wife of the sixth Tokugawa Shogun Ienobu-ko, Ten'nei-in-den, and Twenty-sixth High Priest Nichikan Shonin jointly left an endowment for the construction of the pagoda. The subsequent five High Priests inherited the long-cherished dream and finally in the second year of Kan'en (1749), with offerings from various provinces and a donation from the Lord of the Matsuyama Domain, Itakura Katsuzumi-ko, Thirty-first High Priest Nichi'in Shonin completed the construction. In 1966, the pagoda was designated by the Government of Japan as an Important National Cultural Asset. The structure measures 6.4 meters on each side, and has a height of 34.3 meters. As part of the great undertaking for the 800th Anniversary of the Advent of ouf Founder Nichiren Daishonin, the pagoda was renovated by Sixth-eighth High Priest Nichinyo Shonin, and the renovation work was completed in January 2017.

Carvings under the eaves

The front hinged door

Okyozo (Sutra Storehouse) 御経蔵

The Okyozo *(Sutra Storehouse)*, located on the east side of the Hoando across the Uruigawa River, was built in the tenth year of Genroku (1697) by Twenty-fourth High Priest Nichiei Shonin. In 1973, it was moved from behind the Mieido to its current location and rebuilt by Sixty-sixth High Priest Nittatsu Shonin. The two-tiered purlin-style copper shingle-covered roof is indicative of the Tang dynasty of China. Inside the building is a library containing revolving bookcases that store a complete collection of sutras dating back to the Ming dynasty, and has been designated as a Prefectural Tangible Cultural Asset of Shizuoka.

Junikakudo
(Twelve-sided Temple) 十二角堂

This Junikakudo *(Twelve-sided Temple)*, also called the Ihaido *(Memorial Tablet Hall)*, enshrines the five-tiered memorial tablets for the successive High Priests since the time of Second High Priest Nikko Shonin. It was completely rebuilt in 1960 by Sixty-sixth High Priest Nittatsu Shonin in its present style. In 1969 it was moved from northeast of the Mieido behind the cemetery of the successive High Priests, to its current location, east of the Uruigawa River.

Ohanamizu *(Flower Water Spring)* and Akado *(Spring Water House)* お華水と閼伽堂

To the east of the Hoando, under giant Japanese cedar trees, is a spring that bubbles forth fresh, cold water. Since ancient times it has been called the Ohanamizu *(Flower Water Spring)*. Assigned priests rise early each morning to carry an offering of the sacred water to each Gohonzon's altar. "*Aka*" of the word "*Akado*" signifies the offering of pure water to the Buddha, and the presently existing Akado *(Spring Water House)* was reconstructed by Sixth-sixth High Priest Nittatsu Shonin in 1973.

Kofubo 広布坊

The Kofubo was built by Sixty-seventh High Priest Nikken Shonin on the occasion of the General Meeting in July of 1994 of 60,000 Hokkeko believers who share a karmic bond with the Boddhisattvas of the Earth. The floor area covers approximately 3,250 square meter. It is a two-story, steel-reinforced concrete building with a height of 25 meters, and its great hall measures 1,243 tatami mats.

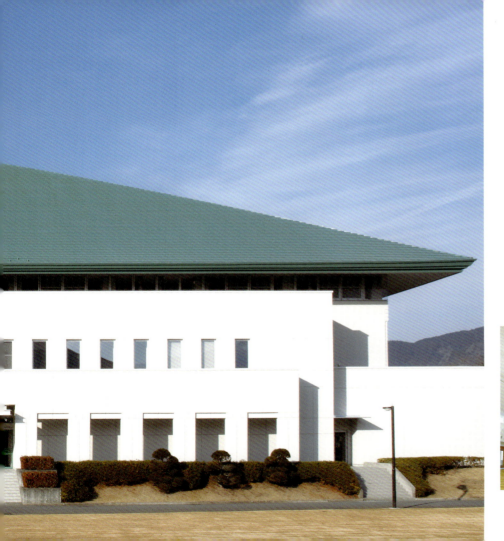

The interior spacious room

Soichibo and Sonibo
総一坊・総二坊

The Soichibo and Sonibo are located between the Somon Gate and the Sammon Gate. The Soichibo was built in 1988, and the Sonibo in 1990 by Sixty-seventh High Priest Nikken Shonin as part of the project to commemorate the 700th Anniversary of the Founding of Taisekiji. The three-story modern architectural structures are constructed with steel-reinforced concrete, and the rectangular copper-shingled roofs take on the traditional Japanese pyramidal roof style. The second and third floors in each of the lodgings are finished with eight spacious rooms, each measuring 240 tatami mats. Members who travel on tozan pilgrimages frequently utilize these lodging temples.

The Soichibo

The Sonibo

Tozan Jimusho *(Tozan Office)* 登山事務所

The Tozan Jimusho *(Tozan Office)* was established by Sixty-seventh High Priest Nikken Shonin in 1991 to facilitate the reception of Hokkeko members who make tozan pilgrimages to the Head Temple. It was originally located on the first floor of the Soichibo. However, it was reopened at its current location in 2011 by Sixty-eighth High Priest Nichinyo Shonin as part of the great undertaking for the 750th Anniversary of Revealing the Truth and Upholding Justice through the Submission of the *Rissho ankoku-ron*.

Joraibo 常来坊

The Joraibo was built by Sixty-sixth High Priest Nittatsu Shonin in 1972. It was originally built to the west of the Kofubo. However, it was moved to its current location in 2011 by Sixty-eighth High Priest Nichinyo Shonin as part of the great undertaking for the 750th Anniversary of Revealing the Truth and Upholding Justice through the Submission of the *Rissho ankoku-ron*. The second floor has a main hall and a spacious room, measuring approximately 893 square meters. The first floor houses a 300-seat lecture hall.

Tokohibo 常灯坊

The Tokohibo was built in 1972 by Sixty-sixth High Priest Nittatsu Shonin. The present Tokohibo was completely rebuilt in 2008 by Sixty-eight High Priest Nichinyo Shonin as part of the great undertaking for the 750th Anniversary of Revealing the Truth and Upholding Justice through the Submission of the *Rissho ankoku-ron*. It is currently used mainly as a lodging temple for overseas believers.

Myogobo, Hogobo, and Jorakubo 妙護坊・法護坊・常楽坊

The Myogobo, Hogobo, and Jorakubo reopened in 2002 following renovations and name changes as part of the commemorative project of the establishment of the Hoando at the Head Temple for the 750th Anniversary of the Founding of True Buddhism. The Myogobo and Hogobo are the temples whose chief priests are responsible for the protection of the Hoando. The Jorakubo is the temple whose chief priest undertakes various tasks concerning the ashes of the deceased including administrating the Dai-nokotsudo.

The Myogobo

The Hogobo

The Jorakubo

Senyokudo and Kannedo
洗浴堂・浣衣堂

Both the Senyokudo and Kannedo are buildings equipped with shower rooms for members who travel on tozan pilgrimages. The East and West Senyokudo, built in 2005, can each provide shower rooms for 30 male and female members at once. The Kannedo was built in 1972 and reconstructed in 2009, and enables 70 male and female members to simultaneously use the showers.

The East Senyokudo

The West Senyokudo

The Kannedo

Taisekiji Bochi *(Taisekiji Cemetery)* and Tenrei-in 大石寺墓地（典礼院）

Situated on a wooded hill behind the Goju-no-to where one can see Suruga Bay on a cloudless day, the vast Taisekiji Bochi *(Taisekiji Cemetery)* contains approximately 16,000 graves on the grounds measuring 109,652 square meters (27 acres), with the Sanshi-to *(Three Masters Pagodas)* at the center. This cemetery was relocated from behind the Mieido in 1969, and the Tenrei-in was built in the central square to manage the superintendence of the cemetery. The structure of the Tenrei-in was reconstructed by Sixty-seventh High Priest Nikken Shonin in 1984.

Sanshi-to *(Three Masters Pagodas)*

Dai-nokotsudo *(Grand Cinerarium)* 大納骨堂

In 1960, the Dai-nokotsudo *(Grand Cinerarium)* was built by Sixty-sixth High Priest Nittatsu Shonin to the north of the cemetery behind the Mieido, and was moved to its present location on the east side of the Uruigawa River. In 2005, Sixty-seventh High Priest Nikken Shonin reconstructed the the Dai-nokotsudo, which is a three-story building with a compartmentalized structure measuring approximately 18 meters on each side, a permanent storage cinerarium, and a communal grave facility, as well as surrounding properties.

Daimyo Bochi *(Cemetery of Feudal Lords)* 大名墓地

The Daimyo Bochi *(Cemetery of Feudal Lords)* is located on the east side of the Dai-nokotsudo. Its name originates from the graves of the "Daimyo," the feudal lords in the Edo period (1615-1868) including the Itakura Family, the Lords of the Bitchu-Matsuyama Domain; the Maeda Family, the Lords of the Daishoji Domain; and the Nambu Family, the Lords of the Hachinohe Domain. Also in this cemetery the grave of Daigyo-sonrei, (Nanjo Tokimitsu), the distinguished lay believer of the Head Temple who made the great offering of land to found Taisekiji is built. Additionally, the graves of the parents of the Founder Nichiren Daishonin, Second High Priest Nikko Shonin, and Third High Priest Nichimoku Shonin are located here. This cemetery, as well as the Taisekiji cemetery, were moved to their current locations in 1969.

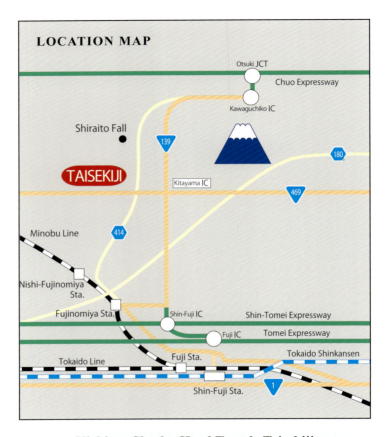

Nichiren Shoshu Head Temple Taisekiji

2057 Kamijo, Fujinomiya, Shizuoka, JAPAN 418-0116
Phone: 0544-58-0810